BASEBALL JOKES

Compiled by Pam Rosenberg
Illustrated by Patrick Girouard

Special thanks to Donna Hynek and her second grade class of 2005—2006 for sharing their favorite jokes.

Published in the United States of America by The Child's World®
PO Box 326, Chanhassen, MN 55317-0326
800-599-READ
www.childsworld.com

Acknowledgments
  The Child's World®: Mary Berendes, Publishing Director

  Editorial Directions, Inc.: E. Russell Primm, Editorial Director and Line Editor; Katie Marsico, Managing Editor; Assistant Editor, Caroline Wood; Susan Ashley, Proofreader

  The Design Lab: Kathleen Petelinsek, Designer; Kari Tobin, Page Production

Library of Congress Cataloging-in-Publication Data
  Baseball jokes / compiled by Pam Rosenberg;
  illustrated by Patrick Girouard.
      p. cm. — (Laughing matters)
   ISBN-13: 978-1-59296-705-6
   ISBN-10: 1-59296-705-1 (library bound : alk. paper)
   1. Baseball—Juvenile humor. I. Rosenberg, Pam. II. Girouard, Patrick.
  III. Title.
  PN6231.B35B37 2007   818'.6020803579—dc22
  2006022650

AT THE BASEBALL PARK

Jake: Have you ever seen a line drive?
Sarah: No, but I've seen a ball park.

What is the best place to put crying children?
In the bawl park.

What runs around the field but never wins?
A fence.

Why are baseball stadium seats so cold?
Because they have fans in them.

Why did the outlaw gang try to steal the baseball field?
Because they heard it was the biggest diamond in the world.

Where do detergents sit when they go to the ballpark?
In the bleachers.

Who turns the lights on and off at the ballpark?
The switch hitter.

Why does it get hot after a baseball game? Because all the fans leave.

Where in the baseball stadium do fans wear the whitest clothes? In the bleachers.

Coach: Why did you show up at the baseball stadium wearing a suit of armor?
Player: You told me it was a knight game.

Why was it so windy at AT&T Park in San Francisco? Because of all the Giant fans.

5

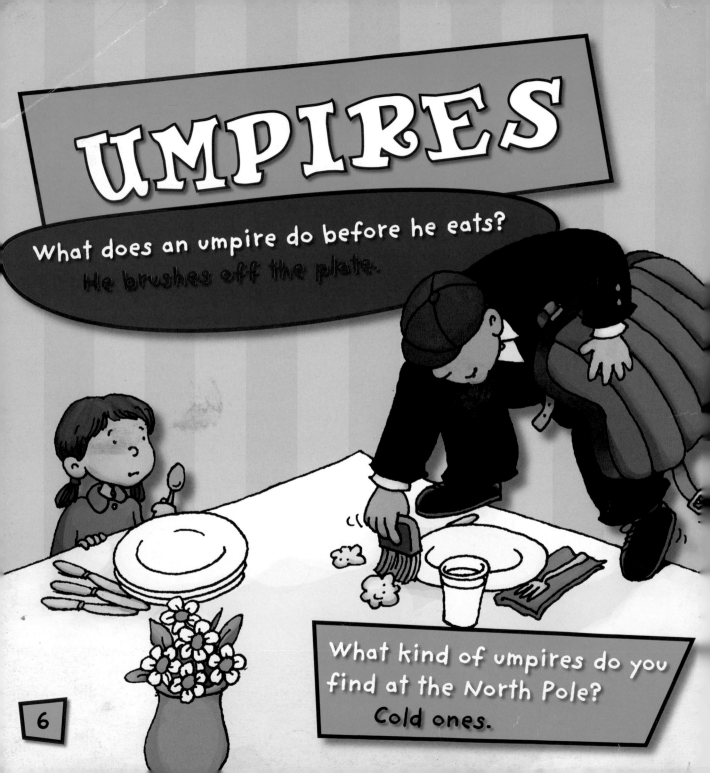

BASEBALL GLOVES

Daniel: Do you know the difference between an old baseball glove and a piece of candy?

Patrick: No.

Daniel: Good. Then eat this old baseball glove and give me that piece of candy.

What has two gloves and four legs?
Two baseball players.

Jerome: Mom, I can't find my baseball glove.

Mom: Did you look in the car?

Jerome: Where in the car?

Mom: Try the glove compartment.

BATS & BATTERS

Did you hear the joke about the pop fly?
Never mind, it's over your head.

Where do baseball
players clean their bats?
In the bat-tub.

What happens when
baseball players get old?
They get batty.

Psychiatrist: What did you
dream about last night?
Anna: Baseball.
Psychiatrist: Baseball—always
baseball! Don't you ever dream
about anything else?
Anna: What? And miss my turn at bat?

Who is the meanest
person in baseball?
The pinch hitter.

BASES & RUNNERS

Annie: We played baseball in school today and I stole second base.

Mom: Well, you march right over to school and give it back!

Why did the baseball player feel like garbage?

Because he got thrown out at home plate.

Does it take longer to run from first base to second base or from second base to third base?

From second base to third, because there's a shortstop in the middle.

What are the best kinds of shoes to wear for stealing bases?

Sneakers.

PITCHERS & CATCHERS

Why was the voice teacher so good at baseball?
She had perfect pitch.

Which baseball player do you need when you make lemonade?
The pitcher.

Why did the campers bring a baseball player with them?
To pitch the tent.

What kind of dishes do catchers use?
Home plates.

What would you get if you crossed a pitcher and the Invisible Man?
Pitching like no one's ever seen.

Did you hear the joke about the fast pitch?
Never mind, you just missed it.

Where does the baseball catcher sit during dinner? Behind the plate.

Two baseball players made a promise to each other. Whoever died first would come back and tell the other one whether or not there was baseball in heaven. So one of them dies and comes back as a ghost to visit his friend and tells him, "I have good news and bad news. The good news is that there is baseball in heaven. The bad news is that you're pitching tomorrow!"

WHEN ANIMALS PLAY BALL

Why is a batter like a horse's tail?

They're both used to swat flies.

What kind of hit do you find at the zoo?

A lion drive.

Why did the umpire throw the chicken out of the baseball game?

He suspected fowl play.

What does a skunk do when it disagrees with the umpire?

It raises a stink.

What do you call it when a pig hits a baseball over the fence?

A ham run.

Why did the frog go to the baseball game?

To catch fly balls.

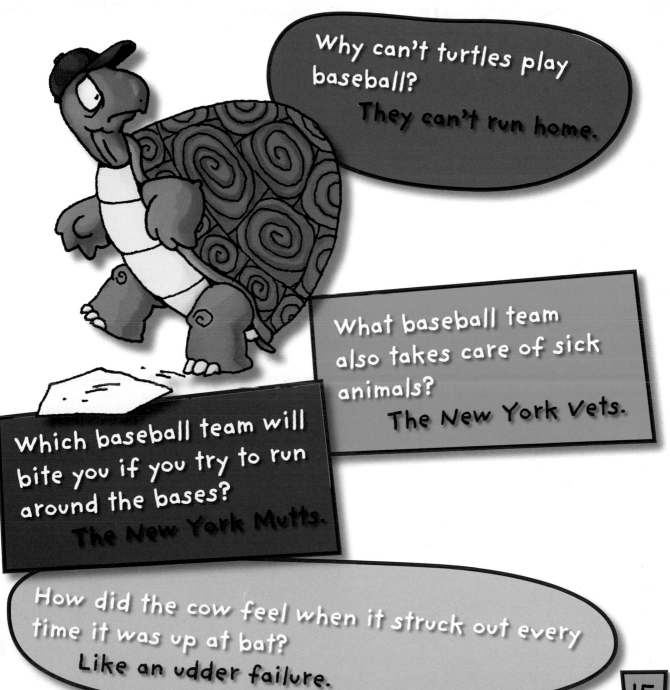

Why can't turtles play baseball?
They can't run home.

What baseball team also takes care of sick animals?
The New York Vets.

Which baseball team will bite you if you try to run around the bases?
The New York Mutts.

How did the cow feel when it struck out every time it was up at bat?
Like an udder failure.

What do you call a dog that stands behind home plate? The catcher's mutt.

What was the spider doing on the baseball team? Catching flies.

Which baseball players repeat everything you say? The Pittsburgh Parrots.

What sport do honeybees play? Beesball.

When dogs play baseball, who chases wild pitches? The catcher's mutt.

Did you hear about the baseball player who was so kind he wouldn't even hit a fly?

During the local baseball game, a spectator was surprised to see a dog walk onto the mound and start pitching. He struck out the other all-star team and scored two home runs. "That's incredible!" he exclaimed to the man next to him. "Yes," said the man, "but he's a terrible disappointment to his parents. They wanted him to be a football player."

What kind of animal do you see at a baseball game? A hot dog.

Woof

What do a dog and a baseball player have in common? They both chase strays and run for home when they see the catcher.

A baseball scout found an amazing prospect—a horse who was a pretty good fielder and who could hit the ball every time he was up at bat. The scout got the horse a tryout with a major league team. In his first at bat, the horse slammed the ball into far left field and stood at the plate watching it. "Run!" screamed the manager, "Run!" "Are you kidding?" said the horse. "If I could run, I'd be in the Kentucky Derby!"

THE MONSTER LEAGUE

Who is the vampire's favorite person on a baseball team?
The bat boy.

Why did Dracula go to the baseball game?
So he could play with the bats.

Why did the baseball team sign up a two-headed monster?
To play doubleheaders.

Where do great dragon baseball players go?
To the hall of flame.

What position does King Kong play on the baseball team?
Any position he wants!

What inning is it when Frankenstein comes to bat?
The fright-inning.

19

Why was Cinderella such a bad baseball player?

Because her coach was a pumpkin.

Why did Cinderella lose the baseball game for her team?

She ran away from the ball.

Why didn't the first baseman get to dance with Cinderella?

Because he missed the ball.

MISCELLANEOUS BASEBALL JOKES

What do you call a baseball player who throws a tantrum?
A baseball brat.

What's red and white and black all over?
The Red Sox playing the White Sox at night.

Why did the batboy suddenly leave the game?
He had to go to the batroom.

What was the twin's specialty in baseball?
The double play.

When was baseball first mentioned in the Bible?
In the opening words, "In the Big Inning."

What did the baseball say when Superman hit it?
Ouch!

What has eighteen legs, red spots, and catches flies?
A baseball team with the measles.

Why was the mayonnaise late for the baseball game?
Because it was dressing.

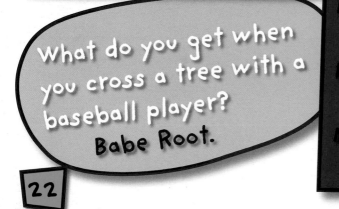

What do you get when you cross a tree with a baseball player?
Babe Root.

Nicholas: Mom, can I go out and play baseball?
Mom: With those holes in your socks?
Nicholas: No, with the kids next door.

The teacher asked her class to write a paper about baseball. One minute later, Henry turned in his paper. It read, "Game called on account of rain."

23

About Patrick Girouard:

Patrick Girouard has been illustrating books for almost 15 years but still looks remarkably lifelike. He loves reading, movies, coffee, robots, a beautiful red-haired lady named Rita, and especially his sons, Marc and Max. Here's an interesting fact: A dog named Sam lives under his drawing board. You can visit him (Patrick, not Sam) at www.pgirouard.com.

About Pam Rosenberg:

Pam Rosenberg is a former junior high school teacher and corporate trainer. She currently works as an author, editor, and the mother of Sarah and Jake. She took on this project as a service to all her fellow parents of young children. At least now their kids will have lots of jokes to choose from when looking for the one they will tell their parents over and over and over again!